Homework Helpers
Reading Comprehension

As a parent, you want your chi_____ do well in school. The activities in the _____ will help your child develop the skills an_____...ence that lead to success. Humorous illustrations make these practice activities interesting for your child.

HOW TO USE THIS BOOK

- Provide a quiet, comfortable place to work with your child.

- Plan a special time to work with your child. Create a warm, accepting atmosphere so your child will enjoy spending this time with you. Provide as much help as your child needs to be successful. Limit each session to one or two activities.

- Check the answers with your child as soon as an activity has been completed. (Be sure to remove the answer pages from the center of the book before your child uses the book.)

- The activities in this book were selected from previously published Frank Schaffer materials.

- Each activity in this book includes a descriptive or informational story on one page and a series of questions on the following page.

Illustrated by Leslie Franz and Karen Nakano

e 2

Homework Helper Record

Color the spot for each activity you complete.

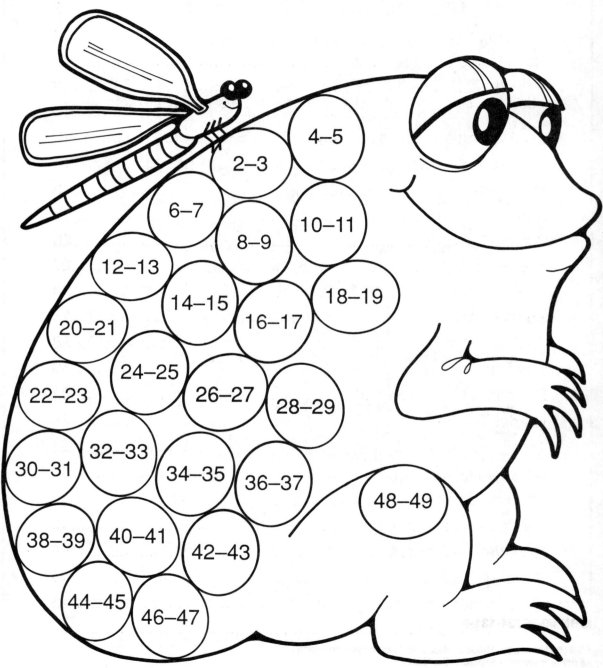

2–3
4–5
6–7
8–9
10–11
12–13
14–15
16–17
18–19
20–21
22–23
24–25
26–27
28–29
30–31
32–33
34–35
36–37
38–39
40–41
42–43
44–45
46–47
48–49

Table of Contents

Saving Stamps

Fred and Tory save stamps. They have four books of stamps. On Saturdays they go to the stamp store. They look to see what is new. Sometimes they buy stamps.

 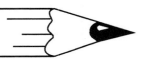

Write Here!

1. Who is the story about?

_____

2. What do they save?

_____

3. How many books of stamps do they have?

_____

4. When do they go to the stamp store?

_____

5. What do they look to see?

_____

6. What do they buy sometimes?

_____

7. What do you like to save?

_____

_____

The Engineer

Manuel wants to be an engineer. He wants to build bridges and rockets. Last week he built a small bridge. The bridge was made of wood. It was very strong.

 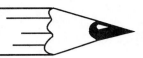

Write Here!

1. Who is the story about?

   _____

2. What does he want to be?

   _____

3. What two things does he want to build?

   _____

4. What did he build last week?

   _____

5. What was the bridge made of?

   _____

6. Was the bridge weak or strong?

   _____

7. Describe a bridge you have seen.

   _____

   _____

Jan's Helmet

Jan has a helmet. It is blue and gold. She wears the helmet on her head. She always wears it when she plays. Jan likes to play football. The helmet protects her head.

Write Here!

1. Who has a helmet?

   _____

2. What color is the helmet?

   _____

3. Where does Jan wear the helmet?

   _____

4. When does she wear it?

   _____

5. What sport does Jan like to play?

   _____

6. What does the helmet do?

   _____

7. Do you think bike riders should wear helmets? Tell why or why not.

   _____

   _____

Soccer

Bob likes to play soccer. He has played for two years. Bob's team is called the Blazers. There are twelve players on the team. The team practices on Tuesdays. Games are played on Thursdays.

Write Here!

1. Who likes to play soccer?

   _____

2. How long has he played?

   _____

3. What team does Bob play on?

   _____

4. How many players are on the team?

   _____

5. When does the team practice?

   _____

6. When are the games played?

   _____

7. Tell about a sport you like to play or watch.

   _____

   _____

Different Drinks

Jenny likes to make different drinks. She uses a mixer to make the drinks. Sometimes Jenny mixes bananas and cream. Sometimes she uses chocolate and peaches. The drinks taste like milk shakes. Jenny makes a drink every day.

Write Here!

1. What does Jenny like to make?

   _____

2. What does she use to make the drinks?

   _____

3. What does she mix with bananas?

   _____

4. What does she mix with chocolate?

   _____

5. What do the drinks taste like?

   _____

6. How often does Jenny make a drink?

   _____

7. What kind of drink would you like to make?

   _____

   _____

Our Fishtank

We have a fishtank in our room. There are ten fish in the tank. We put green plants in the water. We put rocks on the bottom. We put a snail in the tank. The snail keeps the tank clean.

 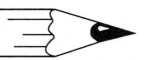

Write Here!

1. What do we have in our room?

   _____

2. How many fish are in the tank?

   _____

3. What color are the plants?

   _____

4. Where did we put rocks?

   _____

5. What animal did we put in the tank?

   _____

6. What keeps the tank clean?

   _____

7. Why do you think fish are good pets?

   _____

   _____

The Jungle

Many animals live in the jungle. Fish swim in the water. Monkeys swing in the trees. Colorful birds fly around. The animals make loud noises. The air in the jungle is very hot.

Write Here!

1. Where do many animals live?

   _____

2. What animals swim in the water?

   _____

3. What animals swing in the trees?

   _____

4. What animals fly around?

   _____

5. What do the animals make?

   _____

6. Is the air in the jungle hot or cold?

   _____

7. Would you like to visit a jungle? Tell why or why not.

   _____

   _____

The Race

Mike and Mary ran a race at school. They ran two miles. It rained and rained on the day of the race. The track became muddy. Mike and Mary finished the race anyway.

16

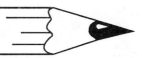

Write Here!

1. What did Mike and Mary do?

   _____

2. Where was the race?

   _____

3. How far did they run?

   _____

4. What happened on the day of the race?

   _____

5. What happened to the track?

   _____

6. Who finished the race?

   _____

7. How do you think the children felt at the end of the race?

   _____

   _____

Summer Camp

Last summer José went to camp. The camp was in the mountains. There was a swimming pool at the camp. Once a week the campers went horseback riding. José wants to go to camp again next year.

Write Here!

1. Who is the story about?

   _____

2. Where did José go?

   _____

3. When did he go?

   _____

4. Where was the camp?

   _____

5. Where did the children swim?

   _____

6. What did the campers do once a week?

   _____

7. Would you like to go to camp? Tell why or why not.

   _____

   _____

Playing Tennis

Joe learned to play tennis at the playground. He took eight lessons. He learned to hit the ball over the net. His father bought him new tennis shoes. The shoes are green and white.

20

Write Here!

1. What is the boy's name?

   _____

2. What game did he learn to play?

   _____

3. Where did he learn to play the game?

   _____

4. How many lessons did he take?

   _____

5. What did he learn to do?

   _____

6. What did Joe's father buy him?

   _____

7. Write two sentences about your favorite shoes.

   _____

   _____

The Gold Watch

Becky's grandfather gave her a pocket watch. It is made of gold. The watch has a long chain. A long time ago the watch belonged to Becky's great-grandfather. The watch is very old. It is still running!

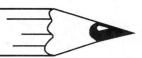

Write Here!

1. Who gave Becky the watch?

_____

2. What kind of watch is it?

_____

3. What is the watch made of?

_____

4. What does the watch have?

_____

5. Who did the watch belong to a long time ago?

_____

6. Is the watch old or new?

_____

7. How should Becky take care of the watch?

_____

_____

Kim's Mother

Kim's mother is a carpenter. One day she went to school. She showed the children how to use a hammer. The children practiced for two hours. Kim's mother stayed until noon. After lunch the children built wooden boxes.

Pull-Out Answers

Remove these answer pages before your child uses this book.

Pull-Out Answers

Page 3
1. Fred and Tory
2. stamps
3. four
4. on Saturdays
5. what is new
6. stamps
7. Answers will vary.

Page 5
1. Manuel
2. an engineer
3. bridges and rockets
4. a small bridge
5. wood
6. strong
7. Descriptions will vary.

Page 7
1. Jan
2. blue and gold
3. on her head
4. when she plays
5. football
6. keeps Jan's head safe
7. Answers will vary.

Page 9
1. Bob
2. for two years
3. the Blazers
4. twelve players
5. on Tuesdays
6. on Thursdays
7. Answers will vary.

Page 11
1. different drinks
2. a mixer
3. cream
4. peaches
5. milk shakes
6. every day
7. Answers will vary.

Page 13
1. a fishtank
2. ten fish
3. green
4. on the bottom
5. a snail
6. the snail
7. Answers will vary.

Page 15
1. in the jungle
2. fish
3. monkeys
4. colorful birds
5. loud noises
6. hot
7. Answers will vary.

Page 17
1. They ran a race.
2. at school
3. two miles
4. It rained and rained.
5. It became muddy.
6. Mike and Mary
7. Answers will vary.

Page 19
1. José
2. to camp
3. last summer
4. in the mountains
5. in a swimming pool
6. They went horseback riding.
7. Answers will vary.

Page 21
1. Joe
2. tennis
3. at the playground
4. eight lessons
5. to hit the ball over the net
6. new tennis shoes
7. Sentences will vary.

Pull-Out Answers

Page 23
1. her grandfather
2. a pocket watch
3. gold
4. a long chain
5. Becky's great-grandfather
6. old
7. Answers will vary.

Page 25
1. Kim's mother
2. to school
3. how to use a hammer
4. at noon
5. wooden boxes
6. after lunch
7. Answers will vary.

Page 27
1. a birthday party
2. ten friends
3. to the beach
4. Bob's dog
5. Sid
6. rolls and cake
7. Descriptions will vary.

Page 29
1. The New Car
2. Pat's family
3. silver and black
4. gray
5. the Silver Star
6. five people
7. Descriptions will vary.

Page 31
1. where it is cold and snowy in the winter
2. on a snowmobile
3. Zack's father
4. to buy bread
5. Zack's uncle
6. Answers will vary.

Page 33
1. equality
2. unfair, peaceful
3. speeches
4. famous
5. Peace
6. Answers will vary.

Page 35
1. a slave who escaped
2. She helped other slaves escape.
3. food and clothing
4. in homes, cellars, barns, and churches
5. a system for helping slaves escape
6. Answers will vary.

Page 37
1. president, Civil War
2. strong
3. speeches
4. Gettysburg Address
5. slaves
6. Answers will vary.

Page 39
1. Sally Ride
2. in 1983
3. the space shuttle *Challenger*
4. six days long
5. She conducted experiments.
6. Answers will vary.

Page 41
1. Thomas Edison
2. three
3. the phonograph, the electric light, and the motion picture
4. He improved them.
5. He worked long hours.
6. Answers will vary.

Pull-Out Answers

Page 43
1. George Washington
2. for eight years
3. He was a general in the army.
4. the Constitution of the United States
5. February 22
6. Answers will vary.

Page 45
1. to the park
2. The cars were going too fast.
3. It jumped on a shoe.
4. The shoe started to run.
5. thump, squish
6. for an hour
7. take the bus

Page 47
1. at camp
2. on a bus
3. to the wrong camp
4. late at night
5. 300 frogs
6. The zipper got stuck.
7. She said camp is fun.

Page 49
1. at a zoo
2. to brush Higby's teeth
3. a giant toothbrush
4. It is Higby's favorite.
5. ten minutes
6. beautiful
7. Answers will vary.

Write Here!

1. Who is a carpenter?

   _____

2. Where did she go one day?

   _____

3. What did she show the children?

   _____

4. When did Kim's mother leave?

   _____

5. What did the children make?

   _____

6. When did they make them?

   _____

7. Tell about someone who visited your school.

   _____

   _____

Bob's Party

Bob had a birthday party. He took ten friends to the beach. He brought along his dog. The dog's name is Sid. Sid ate all the hot dogs. So the children ate rolls and cake!

26

Write Here!

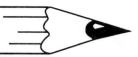

1. What kind of party did Bob have?

   _____

2. How many friends went to the party?

   _____

3. Where did they go?

   _____

4. Who is Sid?

   _____

5. Who ate the hot dogs?

   _____

6. What did the children eat?

   _____

7. Describe a birthday party you remember.

   _____

   _____

The New Car

Pat's family has a new car. It is silver and black. The seats have gray stripes. There are seat belts in the front and back. Pat calls the new car the Silver Star. Five people fit in the new car.

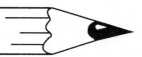

Write Here!

1. What is the title of the story?

   _____

2. Who has a new car?

   _____

3. What color is the car?

   _____

4. What color are the stripes on the seats?

   _____

5. What does Pat call the car?

   _____

6. How many people fit in the new car?

   _____

7. Describe a car you would like to ride in.

   _____

   _____

The Snowmobile

Zack lives where it is cold and snowy in the winter. He rides around his farm on a snowmobile. Zack's father taught him how to ride safely. Sometimes Zack rides to his uncle's store to buy bread for his mother. Zack always gets home before dark.

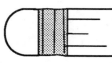 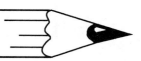

Write Here!

1. Where does Zack live?

   _____

2. How does Zack ride around the farm?

   _____

3. Who taught Zack to ride safely?

   _____

4. Why does Zack go to the store sometimes?

   _____

5. Who owns the store?

   _____

6. Why do you think Zack gets home before dark?

   _____

   _____

   _____

   _____

Dr. Martin Luther King, Jr.

    Dr. Martin Luther King, Jr., worked for equality for all people. He worked in peaceful ways to change unfair laws. King made speeches to tell others about his ideas. His most famous speech was called "I Have a Dream." Dr. King was awarded the Nobel Peace Prize in 1963.

Write Here!

Word Box

speeches	unfair	famous
equality	Peace	peaceful

1. Dr. Martin Luther King, Jr., worked for _____ for all people.

2. He worked to change _____ laws in _____ ways.

3. Dr. King made _____ to tell others about his ideas.

4. His most _____ speech was called "I Have a Dream."

5. Dr. King was awarded the Nobel _____ prize in 1963.

6. How can you try to change something that is unfair?

_____

_____

_____

Harriet Tubman

Harriet Tubman was a slave who escaped to freedom. She helped other slaves escape through the underground railroad. The underground railroad wasn't a real railroad. It was a system for helping slaves escape. People gave food and clothing to the runaway slaves. They hid them in homes, cellars, barns, and churches.

 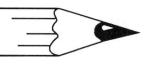

Write Here!

1. Who was Harriet Tubman?

    _____

2. What did Harriet Tubman do?

    _____

    _____

3. What did people along the way give to runaway slaves?

    _____

4. Where did people hide the slaves?

    _____

    _____

5. What was the underground railroad?

    _____

    _____

6. How do you help other people?

    _____

Abraham Lincoln

Abraham Lincoln was president during the Civil War. He worked hard to keep our government strong. He made many important speeches. One was the Gettysburg Address. Another told about freeing the slaves.

 # Write Here!

Word Box		
slaves	president	strong
Civil War	Gettysburg Address	speeches

1. Abraham Lincoln was _____

   during the _____ .

2. He worked hard to keep our government _____ .

3. He made many important _____ .

4. One speech was the _____ .

5. Another speech told about freeing the _____ .

6. What would you like Abraham Lincoln to know about you?

   _____

   _____

   _____

   _____

Sally Ride

Sally Ride is an astronaut and scientist. In 1983 Sally Ride became the first American woman to fly in space. She made a six-day flight on the space shuttle *Challenger.* She was a mission specialist. She conducted experiments.

Write Here!

1. Who was the first American woman to fly in space?

   _____

2. When did Sally Ride fly in space for the first time?

   _____

3. On which space shuttle did she ride?

   _____

4. How long was her first space flight?

   _____

5. What work did she do on the space shuttle?

   _____

6. How do you think Earth would look from space?

   _____

   _____

   _____

Thomas Edison

   Thomas Edison may have been the world's greatest
inventor. Three of his inventions changed the lives of many
people. They were the phonograph, the electric light, and the
motion picture. He also improved the inventions of other
people. He worked long hours.

Write Here!

1. Who may have been the world's greatest inventor?

   _____

2. How many of his inventions changed the lives of many people?

   _____

3. What were the three inventions that changed the lives of many people?

   _____

   _____

4. What did Edison do with other people's inventions?

   _____

5. How do you know Edison was a hard worker?

   _____

6. Which invention named above do you think is the most important?

   _____

   _____

George Washington

George Washington was the first president of the United States. He was president for eight years. Before becoming president, he was a general in the army. George Washington signed the Constitution of the United States. His birthday is February 22.

Write Here!

1. Who was the first president of the United States?

   _____

2. How long was George Washington president?

   _____

3. What job did Washington have before becoming president?

   _____

   _____

4. What important paper did Washington sign?

   _____

5. When is George Washington's birthday?

   _____

6. Would you like to become the President of the United States?

   _____

   _____

A Spider's Adventure

"I want to go to the park. How am I going to cross the street?" wondered the spider. "The cars are going too fast." Just then, a shoe appeared. "Perfect! I'll jump on this shoe." Thump. Squish. Thump. Squish. The shoe started running. It went faster and faster. "Help! Let me off!" screamed the spider but the shoe ran on and on. One hour later, it finally stopped. "I'll never take a shoe anywhere again!" sputtered the spider. "Next time, I'm taking the bus."

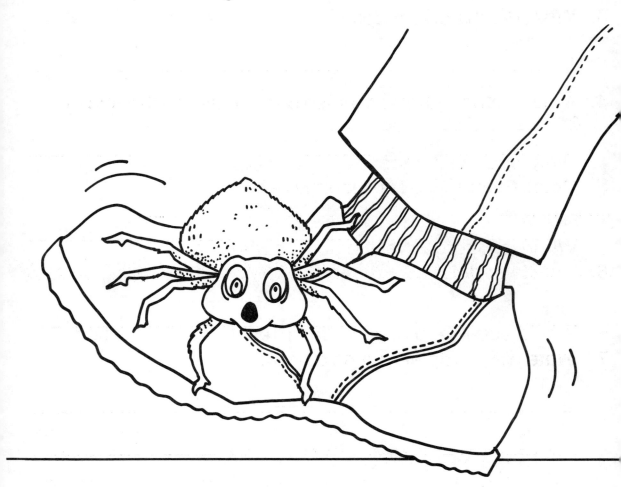

44

Write Here!

1. Where did the spider want to go?

   _____

2. Why couldn't the spider cross the street?

   _____

3. What did the spider do?

   _____

4. What happened when the spider jumped on the shoe?

   _____

5. What sounds did the shoe make?

   _____

6. How long did the shoe run?

   _____

7. What will the spider do next time?

   _____

   _____

Summer Fun!

Dear Mom and Dad,

Here I am at camp. It was a long trip yesterday. The bus driver got lost. He went to the wrong camp. It was a boys' camp. Finally, we got to our camp. It was late at night. I found 300 frogs sitting in my tent. They wouldn't leave. So I left. Guess what happened this morning! My sleeping bag wouldn't unzip. I could be stuck in here forever! Camp is fun. Wish you were here.

Love,
Nancy

FS-8164 Homework Helpers—Comprehension 2

Write Here!

1. Where is Nancy?

_____

2. How did she get there?

_____

3. Where did the bus driver go first?

_____

4. When did Nancy arrive at camp?

_____

5. What did Nancy find in her tent?

_____

6. What happened to Nancy's sleeping bag?

_____

7. How do you know Nancy likes camp?

_____

_____

Open Wide!

Terri works at a zoo. She has a special job. Every Monday, Terri walks into the hippo pond. "OK, Higby. Open your mouth," says Terri. "Wider! Wider! Now I can brush your teeth for you." Terri pulls out a giant toothbrush. She squeezes Plum Patootie toothpaste on it. That is Higby's favorite. It is very sweet. For ten minutes Terri rubs and scrubs. "All clean, Higby! Let me see you smile. How beautiful! Your teeth really sparkle."

Write Here!

1. Where does Terri work?

   _____

2. What is Terri's special job?

   _____

3. What does Terri use to do her job?

   _____

4. Why does Terri use Plum Patootie toothpaste?

   _____

5. How long does it take Terri to do her job?

   _____

6. How do Higby's teeth look when Terri finishes?

   _____

7. How do you think Higby gets a bath?

   _____

   _____

GREAT READER AWARD

presented to

_____

**for successfully completing
this Homework Helper Book**

_____   _____

signed   **dated**